SOLAR POWER

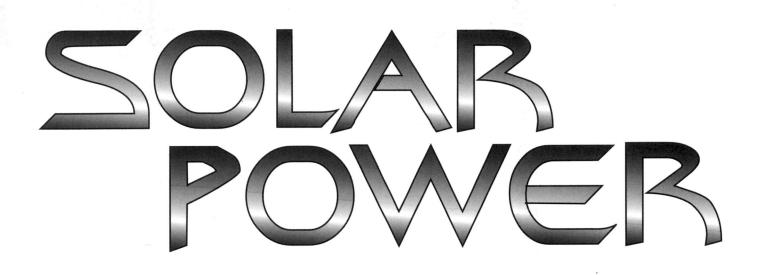

IAN GRAHAM

WAYLAND

ENERGY FOREVER?

Solar Power

OTHER TITLES IN THE SERIES

Water Power · Wind Power · Fossil Fuels
Nuclear Power · Geothermal and Bioenergy

Produced for Wayland Publishers Ltd by
Lionheart Books, 10 Chelmsford Square, London NW10 3A

Designer: Ben White
Editor: Lionel Bender
Picture Research: Madeleine Samuel
Electronic make-up: Mike Pilley, Radius/Pelican Graphics
Illustrated by Rudi Vizi

First published in 1998 by Wayland Publishers Ltd
61 Western Road, Hove, East Sussex BN3 1JD

Find Wayland on the internet at http://www.wayland.co.uk

British Library Cataloguing in Publication Data
Graham, Ian, 1953-
Solar power. - (Energy Forever?)
1. Solar energy - Juvenile literature
I. Title
333.7'923

ISBN 0 7502 2102 X

Printed and bound by G. Canale & C.S.p.A., Turin

Picture Acknowledgements
Cover: Tony Stone/Getty Images (Nadia Mackenzie), page 5
(Mitch Kezar). US Department of Energy: title page, pages 4, 7,
22-23, 22, 32-33, 34, 34 (bottom), 41. Ecoscene: pages 10, 25
(Brown), 30 (Erik Schaffer), 35 (John Farmar). James Davis Travel
Photography: pages 9, 20-21. Frank Lane Picture Agency: pages
10 (inset: D. Kinzer), 16-17 (Don Smith). Ole Steen Hansen,
Denmark: page 13. Eye Ubiquitous: pages 12 (Brian Harding), 18
(Mark Newham), 44 (NASA). Mary Evans Picture Library: page 14.
Stockmarket/Zefa: pages 15, 26, 36, 40-41 (Joe Sohm).
UKAEA/AEA Technology: pages 19, 24, 31, 36-37. Ole Steen
Hansen: 28, 29 (top). Shell Photo Library/Solavolt International:
29 (bottom). James Hawkins/Oxfam UK: pages 38, 38-39, 39.

CONTENTS

WHAT IS SOLAR POWER?

Introduction

Every 15 minutes the Earth receives enough energy from the Sun to power everything on our planet for a whole year! If we could use sunlight for all our energy needs, there would be no need to burn fossil fuels (coal, oil and gas) or to build nuclear power stations to produce electricity.

Yet only a tiny fraction of the energy we use actually comes directly from sunlight. One problem is its cost. Electricity made from sunlight is expensive, but the cost is falling as technology improves. Fossil fuels are so widely used because they give up the energy stored inside them very easily, by burning them. But people are increasingly concerned about pollution caused by burning fossil fuels. And nuclear power produces radioactive waste that is difficult to dispose of safely.

This US Navy off-shore test platform is powered by two different forms of renewable energy. Electricity for all its instruments and experiments is provided by solar panels (in the foreground) and a wind turbine.

Renewable Sources

Sunlight is a much cleaner form of energy than fossil or nuclear fuels. Energy sources such as sunlight, wind and waves are called renewable sources, because they will never run out – they keep on renewing themselves. Coal, oil and natural gas will all run out eventually. There may be less than 50 years of oil left, 65 years of natural gas and perhaps 300 years of coal.

For these reasons, renewable energy sources like sunlight that are also kinder to the environment are certain to become more important in the twenty-first century. This book explores the history, the technology and the future of solar power.

A child plays on a beach enjoying the Sun's warmth and light. Life on Earth is only possible because of solar energy.

A nuclear reactor in space

The Sun looks like a glowing ball of burning gas, but it is actually a giant nuclear reactor. Nuclear reactors that we build to make electricity on Earth use the energy released when big, heavy uranium split apart. This is called nuclear fission. The Sun is a different type of nuclear reactor because of its size and its make-up.

The Sun is so big that more than a million Earths would fit inside it. Even though it is made mainly from hydrogen, the lightest of all the elements, its great size creates enormous pressures deep inside it. These pressures produce very high temperatures.

A tongue of flame curls away from the Sun thousands of kilometres into space. Violent eruptions from the Sun called prominences and flares release huge bursts of energy and particles. A small flare can be as powerful as a million hydrogen bombs, which are man-made, uncontrollable nuclear fusions.

Nuclear fusion

Lightweight nuclei (the particles at the centre of atoms) collide so fast that they stick together and form a new heavier nucleus.

A burst of energy is released. In the fusion reaction shown here, a hydrogen nucleus collides with a deuterium nucleus. They combine to form a helium nucleus and release energy plus a particle called a neutron.

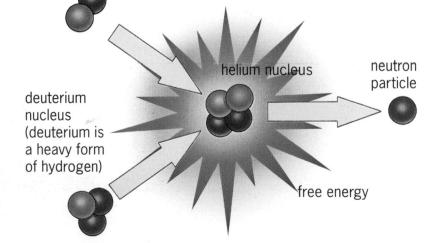

hydrogen nucleus – a proton and a neutron

deuterium nucleus (deuterium is a heavy form of hydrogen)

helium nucleus

neutron particle

free energy

Nuclear fusion

At the centre of the Sun, hydrogen atoms crash into each other with such tremendous force that they join together to make a different element, helium. This type of reaction, called nuclear fusion, releases enormous amounts of energy. Most of the energy is given off as heat and light, which stream out into space in all directions. After a journey of about 150 million kilometres through space, a small fraction of this solar energy reaches the Earth.

Solar energy is a combination of heat and light energy, both of which we exploit. Here, an experimental trough-shaped system of mirrors concentrates sunlight on to a transparent tube. Contaminated groundwater is pumped through the tube along with a chemical that, activated by sunlight, destroys toxic chemicals in the water.

How does solar energy reach us?

Energy from the Sun has to cross millions of kilometres of almost empty space to reach the Earth. Unlike sound, which needs something to travel through, heat and light can travel through a completely empty vacuum. They do so rather like waves crossing a sea or ocean.

Electromagnetic waves

Heat and light are a combination of electrical and magnetic waves. Like water waves, an 'electromagnetic wave' has peaks and troughs. As the electric part of the wave falls, the magnetic part rises. Then the magnetic part of the wave falls and the electric part rises. And so it goes on. The wave continues travelling until it strikes something. Whatever it strikes – the Earth's atmosphere, the ground, a green leaf or you – either absorbs the wave or reflects the wave.

Absorption of solar energy
Most of the solar energy that reaches the Earth is soaked up by the oceans and lands closest to the equator. It heats the large land masses of Africa, south-east Asia and north-west Australia so much that most of the surface water evaporates, leaving dry, hot and sandy desert wastes.

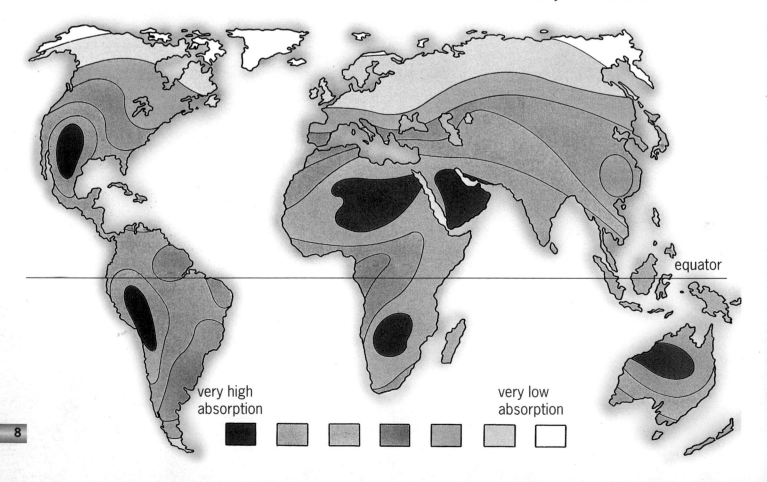

equator

very high absorption

very low absorption

FACTFILE

Light travels faster than anything else in the Universe. It travels at the incredible speed of 300,000 kilometres per second. It travels so fast that we normally see something the instant it happens – unless it is very far away. Light takes just over 8 minutes to reach us from the Sun. It can take hundreds or even thousands of years to reach us from distant parts of the Universe.

One of the most beautiful effects of solar energy on the Earth is a rainbow. It happens when sunlight shines through moist air or rain. Water droplets in the air split the light rays into a spectrum, or series, of colours from red to violet, and reflect the whole colourful arc down towards the ground.

Too much solar energy can also cause the destruction of trees. Following long periods of drought, the wood of trees dries out and can easily catch fire in bright sunlight. In recent years huge areas of forest in Spain, France and in California in the USA have been lost through fires started by excessive sunlight.

Going up in smoke

Wood is a product of trees and as such is a store of solar energy. Burning wood releases this energy as heat. Fossil fuels are also stores of solar energy since they were formed from trees that died and rotted millions of years ago.

Plants are nature's storers of solar energy. Here, trees in the Fraser Island rainforest off the coast of Queensland, Australia, hold their leafy crowns high above the ground. Chlorophyll in the leaves captures the energy of sunlight and uses it to make plant food, a process called photosynthesis.

How does solar energy affect us?

Light from the Sun illuminates the sky and warms the land and the seas. It can also cause droughts, forest fires and cancer of the skin.

The great variety of plant and animal life on Earth and our own survival is only possible because green plants are able to use sunlight for growth. During the process of photosynthesis, plants use the energy of sunlight to make food from water and carbon dioxide in air. Animals feed on plants or on one another.

Solar wind

About half of the Sun's total energy output is visible light. Most of the rest is the invisible infra-red heat radiation that warms the Earth. But the Sun also sends out a stream of protons, which are electrically charged atomic particles (see page 6). Storms in the Sun's surface and atmosphere can cause sudden surges in this 'solar wind' of particles.

When the particles shower the Earth, they give up their energy to the atmosphere, the layer of air around our planet. Their effects can be beautiful, but they can also be damaging. The particles fly along the Earth's magnetic field and dive into the atmosphere near the North and South poles. Here they produce shimmering veils of coloured lights in the sky called aurorae. (The colours in these are the same as those seen in rainbows.)

The surge in solar wind particles also makes the Earth's magnetic field wobble. This can make electric currents flow through long conductors such as power cables, radio aerials and telephone lines. It can cause faults in satellites, interfere with radio communications and trigger power-cuts.

SOLAR POWER IN HISTORY

The Sun as a god

People have treated the Sun as special for thousands of years. Many ancient civilizations believed that the Sun was a god, or that it was moved across the sky each day by a god. The ancient Egyptians believed that the Sun was a god who sailed across the sky in a heavenly ship. The ancient Greeks worshipped the Sun god Helios.

People have not only worshipped the Sun for thousands of years, they have also used its energy for everyday practical purposes. Here, in Spain, maize is drying in the sunshine. Throughout history, the Sun's warming rays have been used to dry everything from meat and animal skins to silk, coffee beans, tea leaves and flax.

Eclipses and human sacrifices

Some native north American tribes and the ancient peoples of Babylon, Mexico, Peru, India and Japan also worshipped the Sun. They all feared the power of their Sun-gods greatly. Solar eclipses, when the Sun dimmed or disappeared altogether as it passed behind the Moon, were terrifying events to them.

Some tribes and civilizations made offerings to the gods to please them so that the Sun would be sure to rise and cross the sky every day. The Aztecs, an ancient Mexican civilization, made human and animal sacrifices in high temples and on mountain-tops to please their Sun-god.

We can tell something about what ancient peoples believed by the things they left behind – their drawings, paintings, carvings, statues, buildings, small objects and sometimes written records. This Sun Carriage was found in Denmark in 1902 and dated to between 1,800 and 1,000 BC. It shows that the people who then lived in Denmark worshipped the Sun as a god.

Mouchot and Pifre's solar-powered printing press consisted of a dish-shaped mirror 2.2 metres across that concentrated sunlight on to a boiler to produce steam. The steam operated an engine that powered the press machinery.

FACTFILE

More than 2,000 years ago Archimedes, the famous mathematician, is said to have used a 'burning mirror' as a weapon. The concave (meaning 'dish-shaped') mirror concentrated sunlight on Roman galleys that were attacking Syracuse harbour in Sicily. The beam of intense energy from the mirror set fire to the ships while they were still out of range of archers. No-one knows if it really happened, but it shows that Archimedes understood how to concentrate the Sun's energy with a mirror.

Using mirrors and lenses

People quickly learned that solar energy could be focused, or concentrated, to make it more intense. In 1774, the English scientist Joseph Priestley focused sunlight with a glass lens to discover a new element. The sunlight was used to heat mercuric oxide (now called mercury oxide) so that it separated into mercury and the new element – oxygen. In 1882 Augustin Mouchot and Abel Pifre built a solar powered printing press. It could print 500 copies an hour of a newspaper called the *Soleil Journal* (literally the Sun newspaper).

The French scientist Antoine Lavoisier built a solar powered furnace that could reach temperatures of up to 1,750 °C, which is hot enough to melt most common metals.

The first solar-powered water heater to go on sale to the public was invented by Clarence M Kemp of Baltimore, USA, in 1891. Solar water heaters became very popular in the United States at the start of the twentieth century. About half a million are still used today in California alone.

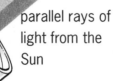

parallel rays of light from the Sun

lens

focal point

On a clear sunny day, an area of ground about 4 square metres soaks up one kilowatt of solar power, which is enough to run an electric toaster or electric fire.

Below: A solar telescope focuses the Sun's energy on to instruments that measure the strength and colour of the sunlight.

Above: A lens brings parallel rays of sunlight to a 'focal point'. All the energy in the light is concentrated into this point. The temperature of anything placed at this point rises. A sheet of paper placed at the focal point will smoulder and eventually burn in the heat.

Using the basics

Solar technology need not be difficult or expensive, or use specially manufactured parts. A collector of solar energy can be no more complicated than a wooden box with a glass top. Gardeners know this particular type of solar collector as a cold frame. Plants placed inside it in cool springtime warm up and grow faster than plants grown in the open air.

If the warm air from the solar collector is allowed to escape, it can be channelled through boxes of vegetables, to dry them before they are stored in the autumn and winter. A sheet of plastic can produce drinking water from desert sand dampened by dew at night. It uses solar energy to make water evaporate. The vapour is then condensed – turned into droplets.

A solar drier is a box with a glass top, built so that air can enter at the bottom and leave at the top. Air inside the box is warmed by solar energy. The warm air rises through the vegetable racks, drawing cool air in at the bottom.

sunlight

glass cover over blackened sheet

cool air enters

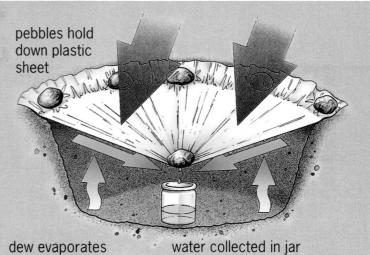

pebbles hold down plastic sheet

dew evaporates

water collected in jar

Water in the desert

A hot desert cools down after sunset. Moisture in the hot air condenses on the cool ground to form dew, which can be collected to drink. To do this, a pit is covered with a plastic sheet before dawn. A pebble weighs down the centre. As the Sun rises, the dew evaporates and condenses on the plastic sheet. It runs down and drips into a cup under the pebble. Cactus juice can be collected too by putting pieces of cactus in the pit.

Left: One method of making salt uses solar heating. Salty water from the sea or from underground salt deposits is collected in shallow ponds called pans. As the water warms in the sunshine, it evaporates and leaves behind a mass of salt crystals.

Flat-plate collectors

A typical flat-plate collector is a shallow box covered with glass that heats water by acting like a mini-greenhouse. The inside of the box is painted black because black absorbs heat more efficiently than any other colour. Water flows through a narrow pipe that snakes through the box, or it may trickle directly over the back of the box. The pipe is painted black, too.

Solar energy is absorbed by the black surfaces, which heat up. They heat the air in the box. The hot surfaces and hot air heat water flowing through the collector. The longer the water takes to flow through it, the more solar energy it absorbs. An efficient flat-plate collector can heat water to a temperature of about 90 °C – almost boiling point.

Flat-plate collectors are used to supply homes with hot water for washing and heating. At the Equator, they are pointed straight up at the sky. In northern countries they are tilted towards the south so that they receive the maximum solar energy. In countries south of the Equator, they are tilted northwards for the same reason.

Sunlight does not have to be very intense to be useful for flat-plate collectors. Water can be heated by solar energy even in cool northern countries. The south-facing wall of this hospital in Torbay, England, is covered with solar collectors to heat water for the building.

In this diagram of a flat-plate collector, part of the glass cover is removed to show the water pipes inside. As cold water moves through the collector, it absorbs more and more of the solar energy that has been trapped inside the box. So the water leaves at a much higher temperature.

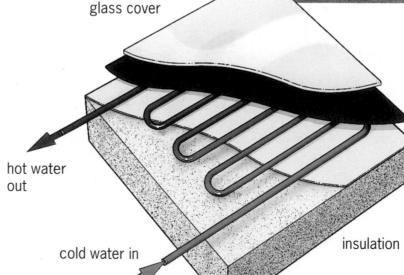

glass cover

hot water out

cold water in

insulation

At an energy technology research centre, a technician checks the efficiency of different types of flat-plate solar collectors. The one on the left has the glass surface removed so the water pipes and insulation layers inside are clearly seen.

Concentrating collectors

It is possible to create much higher temperatures from sunlight than a flat-plate collector is capable of generating. Sunlight is collected over a large area and then focused into a much smaller space. This type of solar collector, called a concentrating collector, can heat a target to several thousand degrees.

One type of concentrating collector is the solar furnace. It consists of a wall of mirrors positioned so that they all reflect sunlight on to the same small area. These types of collectors can be very expensive because some or all of the mirrors have to be fitted with motors and control systems so that they tilt and turn automatically to follow the Sun as it crosses the sky. Mirrors that track the Sun automatically like this are called heliostats.

Curved mirrors or a trough of mirrors that do not have to move can be used instead, but they cannot produce such high temperatures – perhaps 300 °C. This is hot enough to cook food. A dish-shaped collector sitting on the ground with pots suspended above it makes a fuel-free solar cooker.

A trough collector is one type of concentrating collector. A pipe runs the length of a mirrored trough. The curved mirrors focus solar energy on the pipe, which carries water or another fluid that is to be heated.

sunlight focused on to central pipe

hot water flows out of pipe

trough of mirrors

Europe's largest solar furnace is located at Odeillo in the Pyrénées in France. Sixty-three heliostats reflect light on to 9,500 fixed mirrors, which reflect it on to a target only 45 centimetres square. This multiplies the solar energy up to 12,000 times and produces temperatures of up to 3,800 °C.

A solar power tower

When Solar One was built in 1982, it sparkled like a jewel in the plains of the Mojave Desert in California, USA. It was the world's biggest solar power station. It converted sunlight into 10 megawatts of electricity – enough to supply 10,000 people with their electricity.

Solar One was a type of concentrating collector called a central receiver, central tower or power tower. Almost 2,000 mirrors laid out in semi-circles reflected sunlight on to a boiler at the top of a 78-metre-high central tower. When reflected solar energy fell on the boiler, it glowed white hot. Oil flowing through the boiler was rapidly heated. The hot oil was piped away and used to heat water in a boiler, to convert it into steam. The steam drove a generator to make electricity. An improved version of the solar power plant, called Solar Two, uses liquid sodium instead of oil to collect heat from the central tower. Liquid sodium can absorb more heat than oil so does a better job of heating the water.

On the flat desert sands of California, nearly 2,000 mirrors silently catch the Sun's energy and turn it into electricity at Solar One, the world's biggest solar power station.

How the tower works

The central receiver solar power station's mirrors are positioned so that they reflect sunlight on to the tower in the middle. As the Sun rises each day and crosses the sky, the mirrors tilt and swivel automatically to keep their reflections on target.

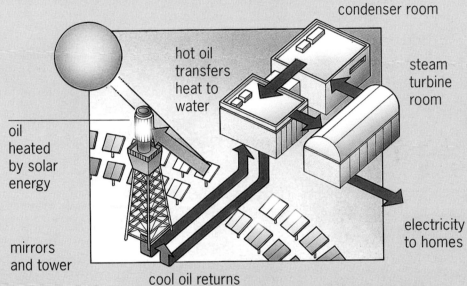

condenser room

hot oil transfers heat to water

steam turbine room

oil heated by solar energy

electricity to homes

mirrors and tower

cool oil returns

23

Satellites are not powered entirely by solar panels. If they were, their equipment would be starved of electricity and stop working every time the satellite moved into the Earth's shadow. Batteries supply electricity when the solar panels stop working. When the solar panels start working again, they recharge.

Electrical power for this lighthouse is provided by solar panels. During the day, the panels soak up sunlight and make electricity, which is stored in batteries until it is needed after dark.

Making electricity from sunlight

Flat-plate collectors and concentrating collectors use the heat from sunlight to make steam, which drives an electricity generator. But there is a different device that can change sunlight directly into electricity. It has no moving parts and needs no mirrors, water or generator to make electricity.

A photovoltaic (PV) cell, or solar cell, the size of a finger-nail produces a tiny electric current when light strikes it. Three or four small cells linked together can power a pocket calculator. Several thousand can power a satellite in space or a solar car. Solar cells produce none of the pollution caused by generating electricity from burning fossil fuels – and sunlight is free!

Solar cells are expensive, however, and they are not efficient. Most convert only about 10 per cent of the energy in the sunlight falling on them into electricity. But they are becoming cheaper and more efficient all the time. Solar cells already provide power for some medical equipment, telephones and water pumps in remote areas where there is no reliable mains electricity supply.

Solar cells are made from a type of material called a semiconductor, usually silicon. When light falls on the cell, it supplies enough energy to move electrons (atomic particles with a negative electric charge) through the cell. When electrons move, they form an electric current.

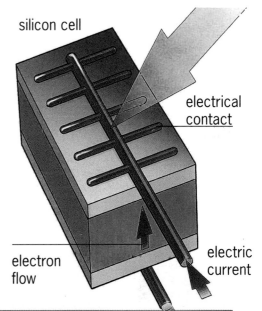

silicon cell

electrical contact

electron flow

electric current

A field of solar panels generate electricity at a solar power station at Carrizo Plains, Bakersfield, in California, USA.

25

How solar energy is used in buildings

Buildings can be designed to use solar energy more efficiently by choosing the correct shape and materials. Gardeners, especially in cooler parts of the world, make the most of solar energy to encourage plants to grow by using greenhouses or glasshouses. A greenhouse feels warm inside because it traps heat given off by objects that have been warmed by sunlight.

Houses, schools, offices and factories can be designed to use solar energy in the same way. Windows that face the Sun are made larger to let in as much sunlight as possible to warm walls and objects inside the buildings.

Modern office buildings, like these in Houston, Texas, in the USA, are often built with glass walls to exploit the heating effect of solar energy. Air inside the buildings is warmed by the Sun.

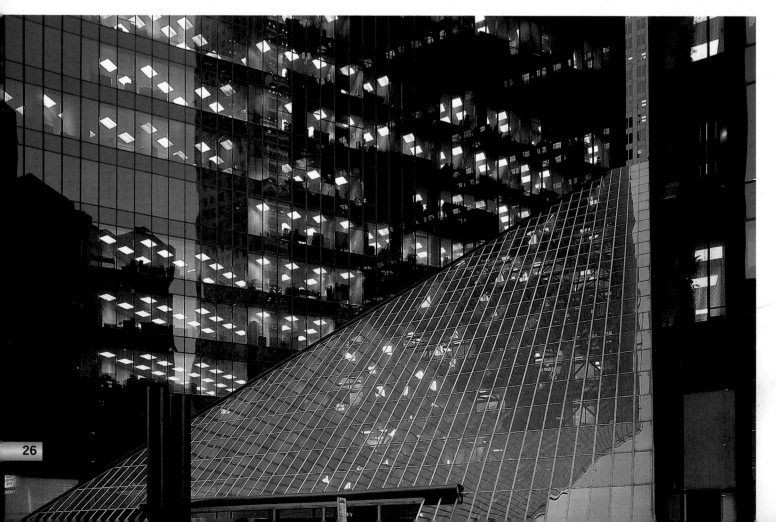

FACTFILE

The world's most energy-efficient house is in Southwell, Nottinghamshire, in England. Rain water is collected from its roof and stored for use. Waste water is used in the garden. Waste from the kitchen and the toilets is turned into compost for the garden. The house is very well insulated, to keep in as much heat as possible. Electricity is produced by photovoltaic panels which generate almost 1,500 kilowatt-hours of electricity each year. A kilowatt-hour is a unit of electrical energy – enough to keep a one-bar electric fire going for one hour.

Windows on the shaded side are made smaller, to stop heat from escaping. Well-insulated walls and roofs help to reduce heat loss, too.

On a hot sunny day, too much sunlight entering a building can make it uncomfortably hot. But used carefully, this solar heating can actually cool a building down by creating cooling air currents. If new homes and offices were built in this way, millions of tonnes less carbon dioxide from burning fossil fuels would be released into the atmosphere each year. Carbon dioxide is a greenhouse gas. It traps heat produced or emitted by the ground, buildings and living things. If too much carbon dioxide is released, the temperature of the atmosphere could rise, with unwelcome effects on our weather and climate.

An energy efficient house. Sunlight entering the house is absorbed and reflected by everything inside it. The light gives up some of its energy in the form of heat.

ground-level air, warmed by sunlight, rises

no windows on north-facing wall

wall insulation

double-glazed windows

solar panels

heat rising from soil

Converting a house in Denmark to use solar energy

A solar home is a building that uses solar energy more efficiently than other homes. In northern countries, sunshine is less intense and the days can be shorter than in sunnier tropical countries. But there is still enough sunshine to make solar homes worthwhile.

Solar energy systems can be designed into new buildings, but it is also possible to convert older buildings into solar homes. Until 1993, the Bille family from Denmark lived in a large old house heated by an oil-burning furnace. Then the family fitted four flat-plate solar collectors to the roof. They provided all the hot water the family needed between May and October. Even on cold clear winter days, they still managed to heat the water to 55 °C. Cloudy skies reduce this to 25 °C. Hot water that was not needed immediately could be stored for up to several days in an insulated tank. This simple conversion has enabled the Bille family to burn 500 litres less oil in a year.

The four solar collectors have to be kept clean to work at their best. Dust and dirt settling on the surface reduce the amount of solar energy that enters the collectors and heats the water. Only heavy snow or the thickest clouds defeat the roof-top collectors completely.

Next to the new water tank is the house's original coal-burning furnace. Further to the right is the new oil-burning furnace that heats the house when the solar panels do not produce enough heat.

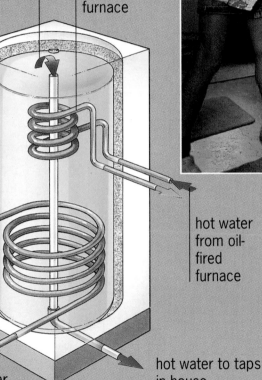

cold water to solar collectors

hot water

cold water to oil-fired furnace

hot water from oil-fired furnace

hot water from solar collectors

hot water to taps in house

Hot water from the roof-top solar collectors flows through the large coiled pipe and heats the water in the tank. When there is not enough sunshine for the solar collectors to work, an oil-burning furnace takes over and sends hot water through the second, smaller coiled pipe.

Some solar houses have both flat-plate collectors and panels of photovoltaic cells, which are being made here. Silicon for the cells, obtained from sand and rock, is baked in a furnace and treated with chemicals before being formed into wafer-thin slices.

Left: These street-lights in Andalucia, Spain, are powered by batteries. The batteries are kept fully charged with electricity supplied by solar panels during the day.

Solar-powered portable equipment ranges from electronic calculators and torches to small fans on baseball caps.

FACTFILE

Nature learned the secret of making environmentally-friendly portable lighting millions of years ago. Some species of beetles, flies, worms, deep-sea fish and fungi are able to make light by a process called bioluminescence. Unlike artificial light, which also gives out some heat too, natural light is cold. Animals use bioluminescence to attract mates or prey (food), or to warn off other creatures. No-one knows why some mushrooms and other fungi glow.

Portable solar power

The most common type of portable power supply is the battery, but batteries have a short lifetime. They soon have to be replaced or recharged. Solar power is one alternative to the battery. Solar panels need not be fixed in one place.

Explorers or scientists travelling in remote areas can take solar powered radios or telephones with them to keep in touch with their base stations. Medical teams can use solar powered equipment in places where there is no reliable electricity supply. Equipment that has to work unattended for long periods can be powered by solar panels.

Solar-powered lighting – fixed and portable – has been supplied to rural communities in every continent. Lighting powered by sunlight may seem a crazy idea because artificial lighting is needed most when there is no sunlight and solar panels will not work! Solar-powered lighting uses sunlight to charge batteries which keep the lights going overnight. All sorts of equipment now use this sort of battery/solar dual power supply.

Solar panels can be set up anywhere to provide electricity. Here they are powering the water pump, filter and heater that circulate, clean and warm the water in this swimming pool.

Solar-powered transport

Air pollution in some large cities is so bad that it is dangerous to people's health. Most of this pollution comes from car and truck engines. When fuel is burned inside an engine, it produces gases and particles that can cause illness if enough of them are breathed in.

Electric cars produce no air pollution. Most electric cars are powered by batteries, but their batteries are heavy and store little energy. A battery-powered car cannot go far before it has to stop and re-charge its batteries. While a normal vehicle's fuel tank can be filled in a few seconds, an electric vehicle's batteries can take several hours to re-charge. A solar-powered car would be as clean as a battery-powered car and much lighter, because it would not need so many heavy batteries.

FACTFILE

In the early 1990s, the Japanese company Kyocera developed Japan's first solar-powered car, the SCV-O. Its 640 solar cells powered an electric motor, giving the car a top speed of 60 kph. The first aircraft to fly using solar power alone was the Solar Challenger, which made its first test flight on 20 November 1980. The electric motor that drove its propeller was powered by 16,128 solar cells stuck to the tops of its wings and tail-plane.

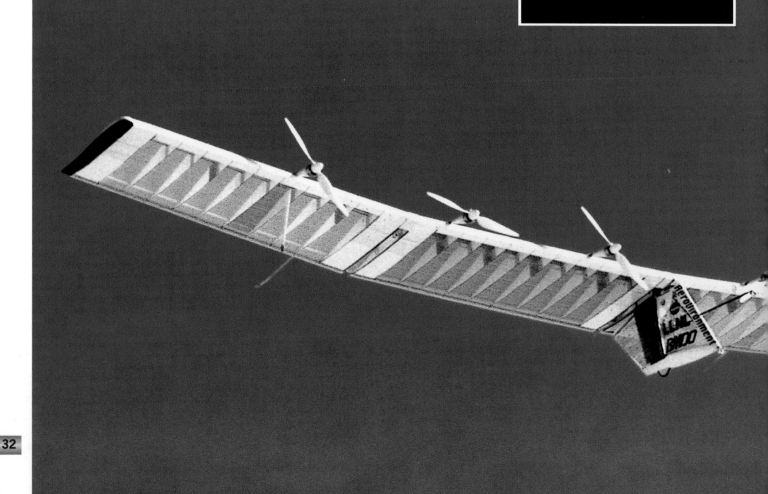

Still too expensive

Photovoltaic cells would be ideal to power a car. They do not use an intermediate heat exchanger, such as water, to run a turbine. They have no moving parts, consume no chemicals, and need no maintenance. However, at the moment solar cells are not efficient enough to produce enough electricity to power a car with a performance similar to a family car today, even in the sunniest parts of the world. Most solar-powered vehicles have been highly specialized and extremely expensive experimental machines.

Pathfinder is an experimental solar plane. Its propellers are driven by eight electric motors powered by 2,800 solar cells on the wings. In test-flights, it has reached a height of more than 20,000 metres.

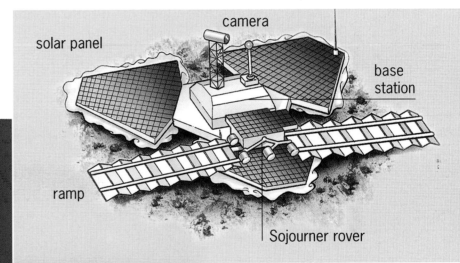

camera

solar panel

base station

ramp

Sojourner rover

Above: A small solar-powered vehicle called Sojourner is about to move down a ramp from its base station to trundle across the surface of Mars. It landed on the Red Planet on 4 July 1997 as part of the Mars Pathfinder mission. As Sojourner explored the surface, its solar-powered instruments probed nearby rocks to find out what they were made from.

A low, streamlined solar car gleams with the blue sheen of the solar cells that power its electric motor. This is "Manta", shaped like a manta ray fish, which won the Sunrayce '95 solar car race.

World Solar Challenge car race

Every three years, teams from all over the world meet in Australia to compete in the World Solar Challenge. This is a car race with a difference – only solar-powered cars may enter. The teams range from multi-national corporations to schools and colleges. The cars set off from Darwin on Australia's northern coast and race the length of the continent to Adelaide on the south coast, a distance of 3,010 kilometres. Races like the World Solar Challenge help to encourage research into solar-powered car technology. Since the races began in 1987, the cars have continually improved, with average speeds rising from 67 kph to 90 kph.

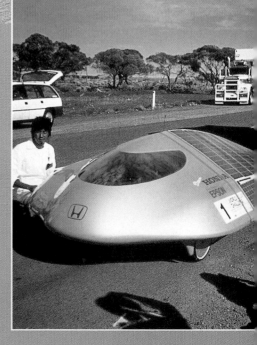

"Sunshark" was an entrant in the 1996 World Solar Challenge. With its streamlined cover off, you can see just how little room there is inside a solar racing car. The driver controls the car with the bicycle-like handlebars.

Sleek, fast – but expensive

Solar racing cars look very different from the average family car or racing car. They are made as small as possible to save weight. Their shape is very important, because they have to be able to slip through the air as easily as possible. And of course, they are silent.

(Opposite) Honda's dream car, for one of the first World Solar Challenge races, about to start day four in the Australian Outback. This car weighed only 125 kilograms. Its solar panels, mounted on the 'tail', produced 1,000 watts of power.

One recent winner of the World Solar Challenge, built by the Japanese car-maker Honda, is 5.4 metres long, streamlined and covered with 4,584 solar cells. It can reach a top speed of 130 kph, but it cost £700,000 to build and there is only just enough room inside for the two drivers.

Storing solar power

Solar energy does not arrive in a steady flow. It rises and falls as clouds come and go, and it ceases altogether when the Sun sets. But we often want to use electricity or heating after dark or on dull days. To be a practical energy supply of the future, the natural peaks and troughs of solar energy have to be smoothed out so that electricity or heating can be supplied when it is needed and not just when the Sun is high in the sky.

While we cannot persuade the Sun to shine longer or more brightly, we can store solar energy that is not needed immediately so that it can be used hours or even days after it was received. Electricity can be stored in batteries. When the sunshine returns and the solar panels start working again, electric current from the panels re-charges the batteries.

At a Japanese power plant, a technician checks that batteries are charging with electricity generated by solar panels on the roof of a neighbouring building.

Sunset over a seashore. During the day, the Sun warms the land and sea, creating vast stores of solar energy and driving the world's weather systems.

Solar tanks and ponds

Solar heat can be stored in tanks or ponds full of rocks, oil or water. Thick insulation around the tanks stops the heat from escaping. A typical solar pond is a pool of salty water, which absorbs heat well. During the day, sunlight warms the water. The saltiest water sinks to the bottom and holds the heat there. On dull days or at night, the hot water can be pumped to a boiler, where it is used to drive a turbine linked to a generator.

FACTFILE

A water tank can store solar energy in the form of heat for a few days. Batteries can store solar energy as electricity for a few weeks or months. Nature's own solar energy stores last far longer. Plants trap the energy of sunlight in their leaves and convert it into chemical energy. After a year or two, the plants can be dug up and burned to release the chemical energy as heat. Trees can store solar energy for decades, or in some cases centuries. Coal, oil and gas burned today are giving up the solar energy they absorbed millions of years ago. Unfortunately, they also give out gases that cause serious air pollution.

Solar ponds

A solar pond has sloping sides and a flat bottom that is painted black. As the salty water heats up, it sinks to the bottom. Cool salty water enters the pond and rises to the surface, where it is heated. There is a constant cycle of cool and hot water.

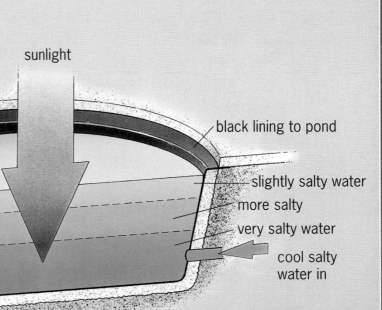

cool surface water removed to condense steam in turbine

hot, salty water out to boiler to create steam

sunlight

black lining to pond

slightly salty water

more salty

very salty water

cool salty water in

sunlight heats bottom layer to 100 °C

A radio station in Mali

Communication is a problem in many countries where people live in small towns and villages spread over a large area without reliable electricity supplies. Radio stations could give out valuable local information, news, health warnings or details of transport problems. They could also broadcast educational programmes, music and other entertainment. But radio stations can only broadcast if they have a reliable electricity supply.

Radio Daande Douentza (RDD) in Mali gets round the power supply problem by being completely solar powered. Supported by the charity Oxfam and NEF (the Near East Foundation), it started broadcasting in July 1993 in an extremely isolated part of Mali where there are no telephones, newspapers or postal services. For most of the people who live there, it is their only source of information about health, farming and changes in the law.

It is difficult for people to keep in touch with each other in rural areas of some countries. Inmarsat, a satellite communications company, has developed a solar-powered satellite telephone booth for use in rural areas. One was installed in Sampa, Ghana, in April 1997.

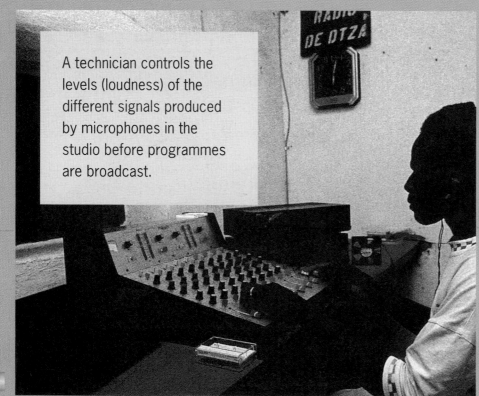

A technician controls the levels (loudness) of the different signals produced by microphones in the studio before programmes are broadcast.

Radio Daande Douentza is powered by electricity generated by solar panels mounted on a rooftop. The radio station broadcasts for 56 hours a week to 168,000 local people spread over an area of 19,000 square kilometres.

A resounding success

Surveys show that more than 85 per cent of the local people listen to the radio station. In the radio station's first six months, the number of radio sets in the area more than doubled. The station is making a real difference to the people. When it began broadcasting programmes about how and where to get children vaccinated, to protect them from disease, the numbers of children receiving vaccinations jumped from 30 per cent to 50 per cent. RDD's success may spawn other solar-powered radio stations in remote locations throughout Africa and Asia.

Bocoum Koumbourou Koita, the voice of Radio Daande Douentza, begins her morning broadcast.

Sunlight-absorbing surfaces

In future, solar panels may be built into the fabric of houses instead of adding them on afterwards. There are solar panels available now that look like ordinary roof tiles. Builders nail them in place just like normal tiles and an electrician wires them up. They are about half the cost of other solar panels because they use a different type of silicon that is cheaper to produce. If one-third of the roof of an average American home was replaced with the new tiles, six hours sunshine a day would meet all the home's electrical needs.

In 1991, eight people sealed themselves inside this glass building, called Biosphere 2, near Oracle in Arizona, USA. (Biosphere 1 is the Earth). They lived inside for two years by recycling all the air, water and food inside the structure. Heating and lighting for the building was powered by solar energy.

Artificial photosynthesis

Plants turn sunlight into chemical energy by a natural process known as photosynthesis. They do this because their cells – their tiny building units – contain a green substance called chlorophyll. The chlorophyll absorbs the light energy and changes it into chemical energy that will fuel all the cells' activities.

If scientists could make an artificial leaf that works in the same way as a natural leaf, solar energy could be much more efficient and cheaper than it is now. Chemists have succeeded in making copies of parts of natural leaves atom by atom. The next step is to put the parts together and check if they can use solar energy like a real plant leaf.

The roof of the Southface Energy Institute in Atlanta, Georgia, in the United States looks like any other tiled roof. In fact, it is covered by special tiles that work like solar panels. They absorb sunlight and use it to make electricity.

Power from desert or scrub land

Hot deserts are ideal solar energy sites. They cover about one-fifth of the Earth's surface and, because their climate is so hot, very few people want to live in them. As the cost of solar cells fall, photovoltaic panels could be laid out over desert land to generate electricity directly. Where deserts stretch alongside coasts, solar power stations could provide the electrical power needed to change salty sea-water into fresh drinking water – a process called desalination.

One problem is the effect of sand blown about by the wind. Sand settling on mirrors or solar panels would block some of the solar energy. Sand blowing across mirrors and solar panels year after year would scratch their smooth surfaces, making them dull and shortening their lifetime. Solar panels and the mirrors of concentrating collectors or power towers used in these harsh conditions might have to be covered with glass or super-tough chemical coatings to protect them.

Solar chimneys could generate electricity from the world's hot deserts. Sunlight heats the air inside plastic tunnels. The hot air rises inside a tall chimney. As it rises, it passes through, and drives, a turbine connected to an electricity generator.

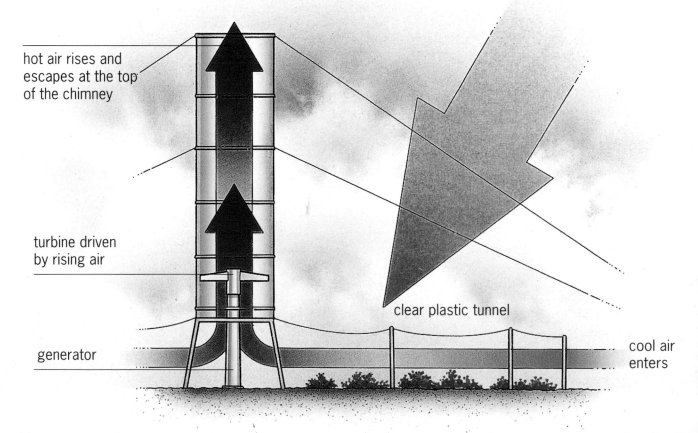

hot air rises and escapes at the top of the chimney

turbine driven by rising air

generator

clear plastic tunnel

cool air enters

Dams built on rivers could control the flow of water that turn turbines.

Wind generators could provide all the electricity needs of a small town.

Robots might be used to clean and replace reflectors that direct sunlight on to a solar tower.

A view of the future
This is an artist's impression of how an area of scrubland or desert could be turned into a renewable energy generating station.

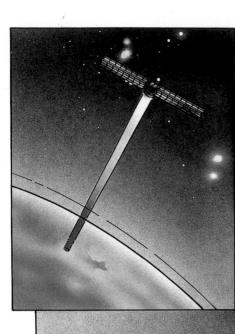

SEPS craft beaming microwaves to Earth

The Hubble Space Telescope, the largest Earth satellite launched so far, weighs 11,000 kilograms and measures 13.3 metres long by 12 metres across, including its solar panels. It was launched from a Space Shuttle in 1990. The solar panels provide electricity for its on-board computer and instruments.

photovoltaic cell
array

Space Shuttles

In future, perhaps when fossil fuels are in short supply and energy costs rise, some of the Earth's energy needs might be met by giant photovoltaic cell arrays, like the one shown above, or by a fleet of SEPS craft (Solar Electric Power Satellites), as shown far left. Each array or satellite would have many solar panels together with the control and guidance equipment needed to keep them pointing at the Sun. A transmitter would send the electricity generated by the panels down to Earth as a radio signal, as shown opposite.

Solar power in space

Sunshine arriving at the Earth's surface is dimmed by clouds and by dust and moisture in the atmosphere. Volcanoes and sandstorms throw massive quantities of dust into the sky. Pollution from cars, factories and fossil fuel power stations add to the problem.

A solar collector or photovoltaic panel would receive much more solar energy if it was outside the Earth's atmosphere. It is technically possible to build a solar power station in space. Huge solar panels would generate electricity, which would then be converted into microwaves and transmitted to receiving stations on Earth. The receiving stations would change the microwaves back into electricity and supply it to homes and businesses in the usual way.

Future interplanetary spacecraft might use sunlight in a different way. Instead of converting it into electricity, they might be propelled by sunlight. Huge sails 'blown' through space by the pressure of sunlight and the solar wind could carry spacecraft between the planets like Space Age sailing ships.

GLOSSARY

Atmosphere The gases that surround a planet, moon or star.

Atom The smallest part of an element that can take part in chemical reactions.

Aurora A shimmering coloured glow in the sky near the Earth's poles caused by the solar wind.

Carbon dioxide A gas made from one carbon atom linked to two oxygen atoms.

Central receiver A type of solar power station which uses mirrors to reflect solar energy on to a boiler (the receiver).

Concentrating collector A mirror or lens used to convert solar energy into heat by gathering solar energy over a large area and bringing it together in a much smaller area.

Electric field An area in which electric forces act.

Electromagnetic Having both electric and magnetic parts.

Electron A particle with a negative electric charge found in all atoms.

Element The simplest substance that can take part in chemical reactions.

Energy The ability to do work.

Flat-plate collector A flat panel or shallow box designed to convert solar energy into heat.

Focus The point where light rays reflected by a curved mirror or bent by a lens come together.

Fossil fuels Natural fuels formed millions of years ago from the remains of plants and animals. Coal, oil and gas are fossil fuels.

Global warming A rise in the temperature of the Earth's atmosphere that may be happening as a result of the build up of gases from power stations, factories and cars, such as carbon dioxide, which trap solar energy.

Hectare An area of ten thousand square metres.

Heliostat A mirror that turns and tilts automatically to follow the Sun as it crosses the sky.

Helium An element formed inside stars by fusing (joining) hydrogen atoms together.

Hydrogen The lightest element of all and the most common in the Universe.

Infra-red Invisible electromagnetic waves that as radiation transfers heat from hot objects.

Joule A unit of energy or work named after the English scientist James Joule (1818-1889).

Kilowatt A unit of electrical power equal to one thousand watts.

Kilowatt-hour A unit of energy that is the same as a supply of 1,000 watts of electrical power for one hour, or 3.6 million joules.

Magnetic field The area around a magnet where its forces of attraction and repulsion have an effect.

Mega- Part of a word meaning one million.

Microwaves Radio waves used for cooking and sending signals to and from artificial satellites.

Nuclear fission A nuclear reaction involving a large heavy nucleus splitting apart, releasing a burst of energy.

Nuclear fusion A nuclear reaction involving small light nuclei colliding so fast that they join together and release a burst of energy.

Nucleus The particle or particles at the centre of an atom.

Photon A packet of energy, the smallest unit of electromagnetic radiation. Light rays are made from photons.

Photosynthesis The chemical reactions in green plants that convert sunlight into chemical energy for growth.

Photovoltaic cell A device that converts sunlight directly into electricity.

Power The speed at which work is done or energy is converted from one form to another. Power is measured in watts.

Proton A particle with a positive electric charge found in the nucleus at the centre of an atom.

Recycling Using materials again instead of throwing them away.

Semiconductor A type of material that sometimes allows an electric current to pass through it and sometimes stops the current passing through.

Silicon An element and semiconductor that is used to make solar cells and microchips.

Solar cell Another name for a photovoltaic cell.

Solar collector A device used to receive solar energy and convert it into another form of energy, such as heat.

Solar energy Energy from the Sun.

Solar furnace A type of concentrating collector that reflects solar energy gathered from a large area onto a tiny target to create very high temperatures.

Solar power station A power station that makes electricity from solar energy.

Solar wind Particles streaming out from the Sun.

Ultra-violet Invisible electromagnetic waves that lie just outside the violet end of a rainbow.

Uranium A heavy element used as a fuel in nuclear reactors.

Watt A unit of power equal to one joule of energy per second.

FURTHER INFORMATION

Books to read

Energy and the Environment by Friends of the Earth – teaching pack (FoE, 1993)

Environment Atlas by Philip's in association with the World Wide Fund for Nature (Heinemann Educational, 1996)

Eyewitness Science: Energy by Jack Challoner (Dorling Kindersley and London Science Museum, 1993)

Fusion: The Search for Endless Energy by Robert Herman (CUP, 1990)

The Greenhouse Effect by Alex Edmonds (Franklin Watts, 1996)

Renewable Energy: Sources for Fuels and Electricity by T.B Johansson and others (Island Press, 1993)

Science Works: Energy by Steve Parker (Macdonald Young Books, 1995)

The Super Science Book of Energy by Jerry Wellington (Wayland, 1994)

The Young Green Consumer Guide by John Elkington and Julia Hailes (Gollancz, 1990)

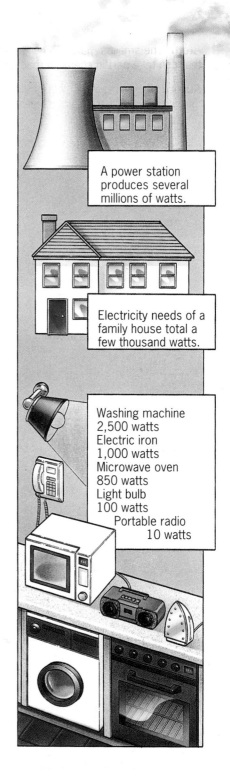

A power station produces several millions of watts.

Electricity needs of a family house total a few thousand watts.

Washing machine 2,500 watts
Electric iron 1,000 watts
Microwave oven 850 watts
Light bulb 100 watts
Portable radio 10 watts

Power and energy consumption

Power is the measurement of how quickly energy is used. It is measured in joules per second, or watts. An electric iron might need 1,000 watts to work, but a portable radio might need only 10 watts. The energy needed to keep the radio going for one hour would run the iron for only six minutes, because the iron uses up energy ten times faster than the radio. The diagram to the right compares the power ratings of household electrical goods and of homes and power stations.

INDEX